A Squirrel Named George

ISBN - 978-0-9949857-5-0

"Oh boy," look at all those tasty looking peanuts.

It's a good thing I came down now from the tree. I am feeling so hungry this morning.

Yummy, these peanuts smell so good.
I can't wait to bite one open.

Out of nowhere a large duck calls out to George.

"Hey, thanks for finding my breakfast, now beat it."

George is thinking...

I hope they leave me some peanuts to eat. I had no food to eat last night.

I am so hungry today.

"Ha ha, good find Patty," the other duck said.

"That little pip-squeak of a squirrel could always find more food. It's ours now," said Patty.

There's no more peanuts, awe...
They ate them all, not even one piece left for me.
Why did they have to eat all of them?

Lunchtime is in a couple of hours.
I will go look by the picnic tables.
I found food there before.
Maybe today I will find some.

(Gurgle, gurgle... rumble)

Roaring sounds can be heard coming from George's tummy.

I have been looking for hours, there's no food around here anywhere.

"George! George! Come over here..."

Looking up, George sees his friend Ralph.

"George come here," shouts Ralph. "Look what I found..."

"What is it," calls out George.

"George, look at this cool soft ball that I found.
Do you want to play with me?"

"What a cool looking ball you have Ralph. What game did you want to play?" asks George.

"Let's play Catch Me If You Can," replies Ralph.

"Awe you caught me Ralph. I almost got away," said George.

"Best out of 5 wins the game. That's 1 point for me," says Ralph.

"Hey, George did you give up? I ran around you 3 times already," shouts Ralph. "I am too fast for you eh? Ha ha ha... I am going to win!"

George with perfect aim throws the soft ball.

"Yes! I finally caught you Ralph."

George stops playing. He is holding onto his tummy.

"Are you ok? What is wrong George?" asked Ralph.

"I am so hungry Ralph. Two big ducks ate all my food in the morning," moans George.

"Ow... my tummy hurts."

"Oh, Hey George, I have lots of food to share, I been collecting food all morning. Follow me I will show you," said Ralph.

"The food is over here George."

"It's just around this tree, come and see George."

"Here is some for you George."

"Thank you for those peanuts
Ralph, they were good.
Can I please have some more?"

"Of Course you can George," said
Ralph, who's eating his peanuts on
the other side of the tree.

Ralph is a good friend, I will just take two more peanuts.

1, 2, there. These peanuts are helping me feel better now.

Mm... yum, yum.

Boy these peanuts sure do taste good.

Sounds can be heard as George licks his fingers clean.

(Slurp, slurp, lick, lick...)

These were the best peanuts ever!

(Slurp, lick lick...)

"Ralph my tummy is full, thank you.
I need to go home so I will see you
tomorrow, ok?" said George.

"Ok, your welcome. See you
tomorrow then," replies Ralph.

What a long day. Thanks to Ralph I can go to sleep with a full tummy. I feel so much better.

More Books Available on Amazon

By Dawn A Harris